IF I COULD
MAKE A SCHOOL

JACK D. FOSTER

Library of Congress Catalog Number: 91-72069
ISBN 0-9631007-0-X

Printed in the United States of America
Second Printing

Center For Strategic
Policy Studies
333 W. Vine St., Ste. 300
Lexington, KY 40507

Acknowledgements

Many people contribute to the writing of a book. In this case, I am indebted to the many people whose ideas have influenced my own in ways I could not begin to acknowledge. There is little that any of us has thought about that is original. Most of the ideas found in this book are shared by many other authors and leaders in education. I can only hope that my views will in turn be shared by others.

I want to thank these individuals for their insightful comments on various drafts of this book: Albert Shanker, Ronald E. Walton, Ray Mabus, Paul Albright, Julian D. Prince, Jack Reed, Raphael "Ray" O. Nystrand, Angene H. Wilson, Gloria Whitman, Richard Boyd, H. Milton Patton, Shelly Weinstein, Arthur Wise, Betty E. Steffy, Roger Pankratz, Doris Redfield, Thomas Boysen, and Debi Furnish. Obviously, they are not responsible for what I have written, but their perspectives greatly influenced the final product.

Worthy of special recognition is Wallace G. Wilkinson, Governor of the Commonwealth of Kentucky, who read an early draft of the manuscript and invited me to work with him to put these ideas into practice. The political courage he showed in advocating a total redesign of public education is rare. Equally rare is the opportunity my service as his Secretary of Education and Humanities gave me to advance these ideas in the real world of public policy and politics.

Finally, I want to express appreciation to my wife Peggy for the encouragement she gave me during the time the book was being written. I also want to thank her for being willing to read and comment on almost every draft of the manuscript. I also want to acknowledge the expert editing assistance provided by Patricia Skrtic.

Jack D. Foster

CONTENTS

INTRODUCTION

One. REMAKING PUBLIC SCHOOLS   1

Two. A CASE FOR REAL CHANGE   13

Three. REDEFINING SCHOOL OUTCOMES   29

Four. A SCHOOL FOR LEARNING   43

Five. CREATING NEW SCHOOLS   53

Six. A SCHOOL IN CONTEXT   73

INTRODUCTION

The initial version of this book was written in 1986. I had been involved in education reform efforts in several states and was growing more concerned that much of what we were doing to improve education in America would have little direct impact on what children learn and how they learn it. We had not yet been willing to challenge the basic assumptions underlying our method of schooling children.

I decided to put my thoughts on paper in the summer of 1986. The more I wrote the stronger my conviction became that we needed to make major changes in the American approach to schooling. The demands on public education had changed but few seemed aware of it. Simply improving what we were doing would achieve only marginal gains. We had to change the very nature of the business. The book was to be a clarion call for changes I and many others thought were necessary to meet the new challenge.

Early in 1987, I first met Wallace G. Wilkinson, then a candidate for the governorship of Kentucky. The unpublished manuscript was shared with him in draft form. As it turned out, we held similar views about what was needed to improve education. The book remained unpublished, but Governor Wilkinson made achieving the vision of educational change it portrayed the central focus of his education reform agenda. I joined his administration as Secretary of Education and Humanities to help bring about this vision.

After 18 months of intense political debate, a bit of serendipity occurred -- the Kentucky Supreme Court ordered a complete restructuring of the public schools. Suddenly the debate about whether to redesign public education in Kentucky was ended. What remained to be decided was the kind of school system we would create. The basic policy objectives we pursued so intensely are now key elements in the Kentucky Education Reform Act of 1990.

Once the Education Reform Act was passed, I returned again to the book I began almost five years ago. What you will read is the book I intended to publish then, except that many of the ideas advanced in the earlier version have been refined in the course of the debate over Governor Wilkinson's push to fundamentally change the way we educate children and the political process that resulted in the Kentucky Education Reform Act of 1990.

Jack D. Foster, Ph.D.
Lexington, Kentucky
April 1991

One
REMAKING
PUBLIC SCHOOLS

The street is warm from the early spring afternoon sunshine. Traffic noisily passes almost unnoticed. Two young fourth-graders are on their way home from school.

"Did you ever wonder who invented school?" asks Greg?

"No. But wouldn't it be neat if we could make our own school?" Mike says as he tosses a stone with his left hand, catching it with his right.

"What would it be like?" queries Greg, as he stops and stares at the sidewalk as if trying to imagine what kind of school he might make.

"I don't know, but it sure wouldn't be like ours!" Mike quickly replies.

Many people agree with Mike's opinion that schools should not be like the ones we have. Changing schools is on nearly everyone's mind these days. The many reports assessing the state of affairs in our schools, mostly public schools, have not had much good to say about them. These studies generally conclude that, whatever schools should be like, they shouldn't be like the ones we have.

Many good things have happened in recent years to strengthen our schools, but how close are we to having the kind of schools we want? The Carnegie Forum on Education and the Economy answered the question this way:

> *Much of the rhetoric of the recent education reform movement has been couched in the language of decline, suggesting that standards have slipped, that the education system has grown lax and needs to return to some earlier performance standard to succeed. Our view is very different. We do not believe the educational system needs repairing; we believe it must be rebuilt to match the drastic change needed in our economy if we are to prepare our children for productive lives in the 21st century.*[1]

Dr. John I. Goodlad, after completing the most comprehensive examination of American schooling in recent years, agrees. In his book, *A Place Called School*, he writes:

> *I do in fact doubt that schooling, as presently conceived and conducted, is capable of providing large segments of young people with the education they and this democracy require, and I include among these young people a significant proportion of those now "making it." There are many things that can be done to improve all elements of schooling -- a more compelling curriculum, professional education for teachers sufficient to separate them from ways they were taught, use of settings beyond the schoolhouse for some kinds of learning, community wide attack on the most dangerous aspects of youth*

culture, and so on. Done in concert, these could make a significant difference. But far-reaching restructuring of our schools and indeed our system of education probably is required for us to come even close to the educational ideals we so regularly espouse for this nation and all its people.[2]

As a close observer and participant in the current reform movement, I too believe we will be unable to provide the kind of education our citizens need for life in the 21st century without a major redesigning of our method of schooling. Perhaps the schools I attended were right for my day, though I have no way to be certain of that. But I'm convinced they are not right for this day and time. We really have no other choice than to make substantial changes if we as a nation want to maintain our technological superiority, preserve our democratic institutions, and ensure that all our children share equitably in our economic wealth.

The Goal of Universal Education

The founding fathers of this nation premised the success of democracy on the electorate's ability to participate intelligently in the affairs of government. Although universal literacy was essential to this principle, it was not a reality in colonial society. Free public schools were founded primarily to ensure a literate population -- at least that part of the population to whom the right to vote would be extended.

As the nation industrialized, an educational system was needed to provide a functionally literate work force -- one that could read, write and "cipher" at a level required to work in the shops and factories of the time. In the early 1900s, most youngsters entered the work force at age 12, so universal education ended with the sixth grade. Only young people pursuing a profession sought an education beyond that point. Private college preparatory schools existed for these students.

Over time, public "secondary schools" were created to provide free access to a college education for those so inclined.

The secondary school mirrored the colleges, with the curriculum organized around the traditional academic disciplines. There were "departments" of English, biology, history and so forth, with department chairpersons similar to what one would find in any American or European college or university. The secondary school curriculum was dictated by college entrance requirements. Rigorous standards for graduation were established to select out those students most qualified for college level work. Students who dropped out of secondary school simply went to work while their classmates went on to college.

We really have no other choice than to make substantial changes if we as a nation want to maintain our technological superiority, preserve our democratic institutions, and ensure that all our children share equitably in our economic wealth.

Universal education did not extend beyond the sixth grade until we raised the legal work age to 16. Correspondingly, we extended universal schooling to age 16 without any clear educational rationale for what children were expected to learn in these four additional years. Ostensibly, the main reason for elevating the level of universal education was to accommodate the change in age of employability. The immediate effect was to extend elementary schooling through the ninth grade. Eventually, "junior high schools" were created to accommodate this new age group.

As we approached the midpoint of the 20th century, the division of labor in our economy increased the required skill level of many industrial jobs. Vocational high schools were created to fill the need for workers with more than a ninth grade

---

education but with less focus on the academic disciplines typically found in the college preparation curriculum. These two avenues to post-ninth grade education coexisted as educational alternatives for the American student until the late 1970s.

The educational needs of the work force again changed dramatically as labor-intensive industries began to give way to information technology and automation in the 1980s. The nature of the workplace was changing again and so were the knowledge and skills needed to be productive in this more sophisticated work environment. Employers were now demanding more than a ninth grade education or the highly specialized job skills being taught in the vocational schools. By the end of the 1980s, a secondary school diploma was becoming the *de facto* requirement for employment in most American businesses. However, the assumptions about universal education or the nature of our system of secondary schools had *not* changed.

Although we have not formally extended universal education to the high school diploma, our present concern about high school dropouts indicates that we are now clearly *expecting* all children to complete a secondary school education. Although the *expectation* is growing, we do not have a system of schools beyond the elementary level that can meet the kind of educational demands we now are placing on our high schools. We face an unprecedented challenge if attainment of a high school diploma is to be the new level of universal education. No nation in the world has heretofore attempted to bring everyone to that level of education.

Recent studies of America's high schools give us little hope of attaining our goal of educating every child through secondary school unless we radically redefine the objectives of a secondary education.[3] The "forgotten half" are those students who neither go on to college nor pursue a vocational curriculum.[4] They graduate from our secondary schools unprepared for either college or work.

Much work remains to be done in the area of *what* children are expected to know and be able to do after 12 years of formal schooling. A more rigorous version of the present curriculum simply will not get the job done. That curriculum has failed as many as half of our children, leaving them ill prepared for life in the next century. We must do much better than that in the future.

The Unfinished Agenda

As I reflect on what currently is taking place in the name of school reform, I am struck by how little of it really comes to grips with what is fundamentally wrong with the American approach to schooling. School reform in the 1980s focused

---

It is now time to deal with the real concern people have about their schools -- what happens (or doesn't happen) in the classroom every day.

---

mostly on raising standards in an effort to improve the quality of education. It was commonly believed that we had not expected enough from our schools and students. More demanding standards for schools, teachers, administrators and students -- the most tangible expression of our insistence on quality education -- were thought to be both appropriate and necessary.

Raising standards in public education is very important. However, if we do nothing more than place more rigorous demands on the system, I believe we will see only modest improvement in the performance of our schools. The "system" will be substantially improved but unchanged in any significant way. The reason should be clear. We can test teachers for competence, increase their salaries, raise requirements for entry into the profession, and require that they undergo professional development throughout their careers, but this does not change what teachers and students do in the classroom, and that's the most critical element of all. Teachers, however well trained, motivated and competent they may be, will continue to do what they have been doing for years.

Many things make up a school, but the most important are what children do and what they learn while in school. It is now time to deal with the real concern people have about their schools -- what happens (or doesn't happen) in the classroom every day. What teachers and students do in the classroom is governed by the structure and workplace culture of our educational system. Schools have not changed, and will not change, as a result of the kind of reform that occurred throughout most of the 1980s. It is now time to focus our reform efforts on our method of schooling and the organizational structure that supports it.

Is There Cause for Concern?

Over the last eight years, I have been both a student of the problems besetting our public schools and an active participant in bringing about change. My thoughts are a product of both. We now have an opportunity to make the school of the future. However, I am increasingly concerned that we may miss this window of opportunity to significantly change America's education system unless we are willing to undertake a modest revolution. We must do more than shore up or reconstitute a sagging but basically sound method of education. We are talking about substantially changing the way we have historically educated our children.

Early in 1986, we were shaken by the destruction in flight of the Challenger space shuttle. The accident drew immediate public reaction. President Reagan formed a national panel of inquiry into the causes of the accident. We grieved publicly at

---

the loss of the astronauts. We searched tirelessly for their remains at sea. When the commission made its report, we became acutely aware of serious shortcomings in our space program. Demands were made that we not permit another space shuttle flight until the faulty booster rockets and other engineering defects were corrected. Although the delay would cost us valuable time in the race for superiority in space technology, we did not believe it was too great a price to pay to prevent a similar disaster. The dollars required were in the billions. Government officials generally conceded we had to do whatever was necessary to get us back into space.

Three years earlier, a National Commission on Excellence in Education examined the status of our schools and determined that they were so defective our national security was at risk.[5] Other studies have since reinforced the commission's basic findings. It will take significant redesigning of the system to correct its problems. But there the comparison ends. No one

---

No one has demanded that we close our schools until we correct the flaws that are damaging the future of our children and our national interest as well. We are expected to do the best we can to make what exists "work better."

---

has demanded that we close our schools until we correct the flaws that are damaging the future of our children and our national interest as well. We are expected to do the best we can to make what exists "work better." In effect, we are asked to continue placing our children in a defective "spacecraft" while the "engineers" figure out what to do to make it safe.

It is imperative that a process and plan for redesigning our education system be devised and implemented before the current interest in school reform begins to wane. However, the changes envisioned here are so fundamental they cannot be

---

carried forward without strong public and political support. The contrast between our response to the space shuttle disaster and education reform is *apropos* once again.

The inquiry into the cause of the accident revealed that many people, both within and outside of NASA, were aware of weaknesses in the booster rocket design. The disaster did not occur for lack of knowledge, but rather the inability or unwillingness of NASA and its contractors to correct the known defects in the booster rockets.

There is an uncomfortable parallel here with current efforts to improve education. Report after report has told us we have serious problems with the way children are taught and what they learn in our public schools. Authorities on schooling have warned about the consequences of not making the necessary changes. As yet we have not acted on the most crucial elements of the changes they recommend. It's time to turn our attention to correcting the flawed design of the spacecraft before we put another generation of children into it.

Obstacles to Structural Change

Our schools are caught in a gridlock of interrelated, interdependent and mutually reinforcing systems such as state laws and regulations, accreditation standards, teacher preparation curricula, and local school structure. These factors collectively determine how schools are structured, what teachers are expected to do, and how and what children are taught. Changes cannot be made in one sector without corresponding changes in all the others. Each can enhance and improve what exists, but none can substantially change the system as a whole. Each of the interrelated parts must concur in any change, and up to now none seems willing or able to exercise the leadership or possesses the authority required to fundamentally change the entire system.

Changes of the nature contemplated by critics of our present method of schooling must occur "across the board." This will require extensive involvement of many elements of the school system, the public and politicians, not necessarily in an iconoclastic or autocratic manner, but rather by a systematic, planned and orderly transition from one form of schooling to another. I believe we can have the kind of schools we want, but we must focus what remains of the energy and concern for school reform on what happens in the classroom.

The Kentucky Experience

As it turns out, we do know how to make a better school. It's basically a case of implementing what we already know about how schools should be "made." On June 8, 1989, the Kentucky Supreme Court declared the state's public school system unconstitutional. Although the initial objective of the lawsuit was to secure equitable and adequate funding for public schools, the high court went beyond the fiscal issues and found the entire system of public education deficient and unconstitutional. Every aspect of the public school system was to be reconsidered and a new system created no later than April 15, 1990. In effect, the justices concluded that a school system in which a significant number of children receive an inadequate education or ultimately fail is inherently inequitable and unconstitutional.

On April 11, 1990, Governor Wallace G. Wilkinson signed into law the Kentucky Education Reform Act of 1990, enacted by the Kentucky General Assembly several weeks earlier. The Education Reform Act reconstructs the entire system of public education in Kentucky. The educational concepts on which the legislation is based are set forth in this book. In many ways, the Kentucky legislation represents the first real hope that policymakers can respond creatively to the challenge to redesign American public education.

The ideas expressed in the following pages are the author's and not necessarily those of Governor Wilkinson or the Kentucky General Assembly. They do represent, however, a rationale for much of what these policymakers did when they embraced the various elements of the Education Reform Act of 1990.

Notes to Chapter One.

1. Carnegie Forum on Education and the Economy, *A Nation Prepared: Teachers for the 21st Century* (Hyattsville, MD, 1986), p. 1.

2. John I. Goodlad, *A Place Called School.* (New York: McGraw-Hill Book Company, 1984), pp. 91-92.

3. See Ted Sizer, *Horace's Compromise: The Dilemma of the American High School* (Boston: Houghton-Mifflin, 1984); Elliot W. Eisner, *What High Schools Are Like: Views from the Inside* (Stanford Univeristy, 1985); and Ernest Boyer, *High School* (New York: Harper & Row, 1983).

4. See William T. Grant Foundation Commission on Work, Family and Citizenship, *The Forgotten Half: Pathways to Success for America's Youth and Young Families* (Washington, D.C.: 1988); and Commission on the Skills of the American Workforce, *America's Choice: High Skills or Low Wages!* (Rochester, New York: The National Center on Education and the Economy, 1990).

5. National Commission on Excellence in Education, *A Nation at Risk* (Washington, DC: U.S. Government Printing Office, 1983).

Two
A CASE FOR
REAL CHANGE

All around us are the products of an ill-fitting school system -- living testimonies to the inadequacy of our approach to education. The social and economic costs are intolerable. It is economically, socially and morally imperative that we have a system of education in which all children can learn no matter what their life circumstance may be. Children who learn differently, who come from divergent cultures and life styles, or who experience life circumstances that make learning difficult. All must be able to learn in our schools.

All children (except the most severely brain damaged) are capable of learning, but clearly, not all can learn in the manner prescribed by our system of education. Most teachers can learn to work effectively with children who have different learning styles, aptitudes or interests; they simply cannot do it within the constraints inherent in our present curriculum and classroom structure. Although it might appear that some children have learning problems, what they actually may have are "schooling problems."

Education authorities seem to agree that the American approach to schooling poses serious problems for a significant number of our children. Many of them fall behind each year and eventually end their schooling without adequate preparation for the world in which they will live and work. If schools are to be redesigned so that all children learn, we must first identify those characteristics of the present approach to education that inhibit learning or that promote the learning of things we find dysfunctional later on in life. Let's begin this inquiry with an examination of some of the assumptions that have shaped our present approach to schools and learning.

The Bureaucratic Model of Schooling

We know that students learn differently and the rate of learning may vary from time to time. A classroom in which children "group" learn -- where everyone is doing the same thing at the same time -- is not one that easily can be adapted to individual differences in either learning style or ease. However, the typical school regimen is built around instruction, daily lesson plans, rigidly scheduled instructional periods, and common materials. The school day is divided into time periods that often have little relationship to the actual time needed to cover certain material and do not take into account different learning styles, stamina and other factors that affect learning. The impact of such a structure on how students learn is obvious.

The learning process that characterizes many if not most of our classrooms today consists mainly of students memorizing (partially and temporarily) somebody else's answers to somebody else's questions.[1] It seems from the teacher's perspective the primary objective is to "cover the material." From the students' perspective the primary objective is to study for tests and then "It's over," meaning they can now forget what they studied. What is learned is only relevant to passing tests.

A CASE FOR REAL CHANGE

Neil Postman and Charles Weingartner describe the typical classroom this way:

> *... what students mostly do in class is guess what the teacher wants them to say. Constantly, they must try to supply "The Right Answer." It does not seem to matter if the subject is English or history or science; mostly, students do the same things. And since it is indisputably (if not publicly) recognized that the ostensible "content" of such courses is rarely remembered beyond the last quiz (in which you are required to remember only 65 percent of what you were told), it is safe to say that just about the only learning that occurs in classrooms is that which is communicated by the structure of the classroom itself.*[2]

In many ways, our method of schooling resembles a manufacturing process. Spend a little time in a typical metal fabrication shop and you will see what I mean. Raw materials are fed into an extrusion machine consisting of a series of dies. As the material passes through each die, it is shaped a little more according to the pattern drawn up by the engineers. Along the way, some pieces don't go through the die as they should and are cast aside. Someone comes along to pick up the castoffs to see if any are salvageable. Some pieces will be recast and run through the process again. Others will be thrown aside as scrap.

Children come into the schooling process like raw material and are "processed" through a series of carefully designed and uniformly standardized "dies" that are age graded and increasingly more demanding. Some children don't make it through one or more of the dies and fall out of the system (something we call "flunking"). The machine (school) can only work with material for which it was designed. It cannot adapt to "irregular" materials. The machine is not faulted for any misfits it produces. The material the machine processes is supposed to be in a form it can accept. In other words, the fault lies with the material -- in this case, the student -- not with the machine (school).

Clearly, there can't be much diversity in ability, motivation and background among students in this kind of school. Slower students may need more time than is scheduled to grasp certain concepts while brighter students cover the material quickly and are bored. Teachers must cover mandated curriculum material on schedule or the whole class falls behind. Students who miss a class are often told, "The material was covered already; we can't go back to it."

Over the years, we have come to realize that some children did not fit the schools we have. Our response has been to build different "extrusion machines" for gifted and talented, economically disadvantaged, bilingual and disabled children. In many states, more than two of every five school children presently qualify for some form of nontraditional educational treatment. Every special class or program we create is an admission that the "basic system" doesn't work for someone. Clearly, far too many children do not fit the mold of the basic school system. Yet, even with these special efforts, a substantial number of children still underachieve or eventually quit school.

The Historical Focus on Teaching

The American approach to schooling is based on the premise that children would not learn if someone did not teach them. Teaching, therefore, has become the central activity in the American classroom. Our approach to schooling ties learning to the presence of a teacher, so both the school and the educational process are organized around a teacher. The difference between focusing on the learner or the teacher happens to be a very important difference.

Contrary to common practice in this country, most contemporary authorities on schooling believe schools should be places where children come to learn rather than to be taught. Schools should be places where learning occurs in a natural fashion, much like it did before formal schooling began -- *because through* curiosity, exploration, asking questions, observation, experimentation (trial and error), and later on through reading. Children should be encouraged to take responsibility for their own learning and not wait to be "taught" by someone else. Unfortunately, our method of schooling is not designed to let children learn on their own. They must wait to be taught by a teacher and then they learn only what is taught.

As it turns out, making the teacher rather than the learner the central focus of schooling may have contributed more than anything else to the undoing of our schools.

Many of us have heard teachers say, "I taught that in class but he just didn't learn it." Such a statement clearly shows that even teachers recognize that teaching doesn't necessarily result in learning. Learning and teaching are not just two sides of the same coin. What people do in a classroom depends mainly on whether the classroom is organized to promote teaching or learning. As it turns out, making the teacher rather than the learner the central focus of schooling may have contributed more than anything else to the undoing of our schools.

Most of us eventually begin to learn on our own as adults, but we could have been learning that way all along. And it would have been better for us had we done so. Arthur J. Lewis maintains that "the ultimate goal of education is to shift to the individual the burden of pursuing his or her own education. To cope with emerging global problems, people will need to continue learning throughout their lives. Their survival will depend on it."[3]

The Focus on Teaching Impedes Curriculum Reform

An educational system built on the assumption that children will not learn unless they are taught also implies that teachers (or at least the textbooks used) have all the knowledge we want to transmit to the student. The problem lies not with teachers or textbook publishers, but rather is due to the knowledge "explosion" we have experienced in the last half of this century. A teacher-focused approach to learning severely limits the domain of knowledge to which a student will be exposed. Teachers can only teach what they know or what is in the textbook. Therefore, what students are likely to learn is limited to the knowledge teachers and textbooks possess. There is little room for students to go beyond the boundaries of knowledge established by this finite system.

Under the present system, the teacher is the primary source of learning. Teachers are trained to teach the specific courses that make up the curriculum. In order to train all teachers in a competent manner, there must be consensus on precisely what they will teach. Furthermore, to prepare these teachers to teach the same things, the curriculum must be standardized for all schools. Finally, since all teachers must be certified to teach the curriculum, the certification system must match the curriculum.

A major change in curriculum usually requires retraining those who now teach similar or related subjects; sometimes it even requires a new certification. In the latter case, state regulators have to create new certification categories and specify the appropriate educational requirements to teach the new courses. Colleges and universities in turn must change their curriculum so that the students they prepare to teach these new courses can be certified.

The conservatism inherent in this arrangement means that curriculum innovation is discouraged, updating of the curriculum is postponed as long as possible and new ways to teach are hard to implement. No one is going to force this much change unless the proposed curriculum change has broad support. A local school that wants to change its curriculum finds itself swimming upstream against a very strong current.

Textbooks are the Primary Source of Information

Our students are not only teacher dependent, they also are textbook dependent. The heart of today's curriculum is the classroom textbook and related materials -- manuals, examinations and other teaching aids. Most schools are heavily dependent on this kind of support for their teachers and the curriculum.

Basically, our schools select their textbooks from what is available from textbook publishers. Although publishers attempt to follow changes in curriculum as they occur, they rarely attempt to innovate on the existing curriculum. Arguably, it is not their role to determine what schools should teach; their role is to provide suitable materials for courses that already exist. This means that new textbooks are not developed until present courses are changed or new courses are created.

On the other hand, textbook publishers are very reluctant to prepare a new textbook for a course that is offered in only a small number of schools. In fact, they have been accused of catering only to the desires of a select number of large state systems where the adoption of a textbook can immediately ensure its financial success.[4] The situation is further complicated in those states that require local schools to use textbooks that have been approved by a state textbook commission.

Even the very best textbooks may be as much as ten years out of date before they are replaced in the classroom -- a situation that is probably unavoidable but unacceptable. Typically, a publisher needs up to five years to take a new

---

textbook from design, research and writing, through printing, to availability on the market. Schools usually adopt a textbook for a period of four or five years, largely due to its considerable cost and the time required for teachers to adapt their lesson plans, classroom preparation and so forth. Inevitably, many textbooks are out of date the day they hit our classrooms.

Textbooks have their critics among educators, but my concern is that we continue to use them at all. Mortimer J. Adler, in his *Paideia Proposal*, urges us to replace our traditional textbooks with original source materials such as books and works of human artistry. The books can be of every kind -- historical,

---

Even the very best textbooks may be as much as ten years out of date before they are replaced in the classroom -- a situation that is probably unavoidable but unacceptable.

---

scientific, philosophical, poetry, stories, essays. The products of human artistry might include individual pieces of music, of visual art, plays, and productions in dance, film or television.[5] The information to be learned in school can be found in its natural habitat -- newspapers, magazines, on the street, in stores, woods, zoos, libraries -- literally everywhere.

A Limiting and Outdated Curriculum

As one might expect, the curriculum found in most schools today is designed to be taught rather than learned through independent study by children in charge of their own learning. The typical curriculum consists of courses or subjects that students take as they progress from grade to grade. Some are required; others are elective. Everything students are taught is found in the curriculum since the curriculum is what teachers teach. A teacher covers a measured portion of the curriculum each day according to a schedule.

This type of curriculum is not suitable for a classroom where students are encouraged to learn as much as they can without regard to the abilities of their peers. In a system where students must learn in unison, the intellectual level of the material learned is determined by what a typical student can complete within the school term or by what someone thinks should be covered. In most cases, little is known about what a student actually learns in a course.

Students able to learn at a more rapid rate find the material unchallenging while less able students struggle to keep up. Teachers may make additional assignments for the brighter student or give special attention to the slower student, but neither is easily done in the kind of classroom found in most schools. The traditional curriculum does not easily accommodate to differences in student ability or motivation to learn.

The subject orientation of the curriculum is also problematic. As most of us will remember from our own school days, the major objective of this kind of schooling is to learn "subject matter" organized into "courses." These courses make up the curriculum. Children earn a grade for each course which is presumed to summarize how well they learned the material. Such an approach to learning tends to focus on memorizing information rather than improving the ability to develop, analyze and properly use information.

The division of subject matter in the present school curriculum mirrors the academic disciplines that defined the domains of intellectual inquiry centuries ago. Knowledge in its natural state has no similar boundaries. The world as we know it is not divided into history, English, economics, political science and so forth.

What is perhaps more to the point, in the first 12 years of schooling we are not preparing our young people as specialists in academic disciplines. Partitioning learning according to academic disciplines seriously impedes a student's ability to see and understand the relatedness of everything that exists. Students should come to understand the total context in which ideas and concepts exist, rather than learn them as discrete pieces of information that are independent of each other.

The mass of information available today means that teachers and textbook writers must select the most important information and make sure that it is covered during the course. The result is an exercise in "trivial pursuit" rather than a thoughtful mastery of the great ideas that have advanced our understanding of the world. Grant Wiggins calls this a "thoughtless education."

> *In a thoughtless education, students have no control over what they learn and how they learn it. They are taught at, told merely to note and apply facts or formulae. Mathematics then becomes like routine assembly-line work. ("Plug in the equation.") Science labs become like cooking courses with simple recipes and predictable outcomes. Physics becomes a metaphysical catechism. Writing gets reduced to rigid rules. ("Every essay must be a five-paragraph, six-sentence-to-a-paragraph essay.")*[6]

Another problem is the difficulty encountered in trying to keep the curriculum current. Critics of American education call for a dynamic curriculum -- one that is ever renewing as information grows and new skills emerge. A 21st century curriculum has to keep in step with a constantly changing world in which knowledge is growing exponentially. Yet, the structure of the curriculum in American schools today is not easily changed.

The curriculum found almost everywhere in America is focused on subject matter and academic content, not on the valued learning outcomes of a discipline and certainly not on the concepts that stretch across academic specialties. The curriculum is organized in a fashion that requires it to be "taught" in order to be learned; it is not flexible enough to accommodate individual learning styles, and it is much too difficult to change.

Schools are not User Friendly

Our present approach to schooling poses serious problems for a significant number of our children. The poor academic performance of these children often is attributed to various factors outside the classroom walls, such as a lack of parental interest, subcultural and language differences, poverty and the like. Children with these characteristics are described in the education literature as "children at risk" of failure in our schools. In effect, they are children who "don't fit the system."

The schools we now have clearly are not meeting the learning needs of a culturally and economically diverse population.

Educators generally agree that factors outside the school can affect learning. However, schools shouldn't let children fail to learn just because they come to school with personal or family problems.

Large numbers of children come to school hungry, physically ill, abused, neglected or under family stress. Such children generally have difficulty concentrating on school matters and often lose their interest in learning. The result is excessive absenteeism, low grades and sometimes academic failure. I believe many of these children could be saved from this outcome if our schools were better able to meet their special learning needs during a time of disruption in their personal lives.

Cultural and lifestyle differences can negatively influence a child's learning in the traditional American school. Many

---

children live in one cultural world at school and a vastly different one at home. The number of children living in poverty and often homeless is steadily growing. Important changes in the racial and ethnic demographics of our schools also are occurring. The dominant cultural minority in our society soon will be Hispanic -- a fact of significant cultural and linguistic importance to our schools.

We always have been a pluralistic society, so cross cultural differences are not a new circumstance. Officially, we cherish our differences in culture, values, sensitivities and religious beliefs. We believe there is a natural beauty in diversity. In light of our acceptance and almost reverence of diversity, it is incongruous that our schools should have so much difficulty with it. The schools we now have clearly are not meeting the learning needs of a culturally and economically diverse population.

Our society also is undergoing significant structural changes in family and family life-styles. American educators commonly believe they should be able to depend upon families to help children learn. Somewhere in our collective psyche there exists this nostalgic picture of little children sitting around a kitchen table with their mother peering over their shoulders as they studiously do their homework assignment of the day. I'm not sure how far back we need to reach in our national memory to find this scene, but it surely is more appropriate to a Norman Rockwell portrait than to any home we may find today. In spite of evidence to the contrary, our schools continue to operate as though such a relationship exists between school and family. The reality is so vastly different.

Increasingly typical is the single-parent family with a working head-of-household. The majority of these single-parent households are at or below the poverty level. Survival is paramount. Education may be highly valued, but little time or energy is left at the end of a working day for such parents to devote to the academic pursuits of their children. We are told that more and more children will be going to day care, then to school, and back to day care again before going home at the end of their day. Others will make their own way home with a house key around their neck to fend for themselves until mom and/or dad can join them.

Schools need to adjust to this reality if we are to provide meaningful learning opportunities for all children. It just isn't realistic to assume that the family can be counted on to help prepare children for school. Many still do, but the number who don't or can't seems to be growing. The school has to

---

The time is long past for this nation to recognize the importance of having a school system that can adapt to the realities of the society it serves.

---

accommodate to this fact of life. Long-standing practices like homework and parent-teacher conferences must be reevaluated. Perhaps now, more than ever, the school must provide the motivation to learn.

In a society like ours, it can be expected that every day some children will come to school with circumstances in life that adversely affect their learning. Furthermore, many of the conditions blamed for schooling difficulties have always existed in our society, and unfortunately will likely continue to exist for many years to come. It would be foolhardy indeed to believe that schools have either the resources or the ability to ameliorate every problem that a child might encounter. On the other hand, schools can do more than they do to help such children. We must help children reach their greatest potential for learning by developing within our schools and communities the resources needed to overcome any environmental disadvantage they may have.

Much can be done to improve the child's ability and opportunity to learn within the school itself. Surely we can make our schools more "user friendly." We can establish a school regimen that can adjust to changes in a child's learning situation and a curriculum that is flexible enough to accommodate to the learning styles and cultural differences of every child. The time is long past for this nation to recognize the importance of having a school system that can adapt to the realities of the society it serves.

Accountability for Learning

Historically, *all* children were not expected to master the entire curriculum. Universal education in practice came to mean universal *opportunity* -- not universal *achievement*. Secondary schools in particular were expected to sift and sort out the unmotivated and poor performing students in favor of those with some promise of academic excellence. In fact, the academic failure of a certain percentage of students was to be expected. An outcome different from this could be interpreted as a lack of academic rigor.

In a world where "quality" has come to mean "zero defects," policymakers are not interested any longer in how students *as a group* are doing "on the average." The public wants to know how near we are to having *all* students learning at the highest level of their capability. Of particular interest here is the weight the Kentucky Supreme Court justices gave to student outcomes in their unprecedented judicial decision. The Supreme Court opinion cited various data, including nationally normed test results, which the justices regarded as evidence that Kentucky students overall failed to receive an "adequate" education as required by the state constitution. The justices concluded that a school system in which a significant number of children receive an inadequate education or ultimately fail is inherently inequitable and unconstitutional.

The debate over the extent to which schools can overcome external circumstances that adversely affect learning will continue in the years to come, but policymakers in Kentucky and elsewhere believe sufficient evidence exists that schools *can* be more effective with children who currently fail or drop out than was previously thought possible. In fact, they are coming to believe that many children are "at risk" of school failure primarily because of an outmoded method of schooling.

The Case for Redesigning Schools

Thoughtful people are questioning the very premises on which our present educational system is based. The present structure of public education is based on assumptions that are faulty or outdated and contribute collectively to the failure of the schools to educate all children. What we need now is a mental picture of what a redesigned school system might be like. The remainder of this book is dedicated to a discussion of what a school could be like if the fundamental assumptions addressed in this chapter were altered to provide a different image of a school and what goes on inside of it.

Notes to Chapter Two.

1.   Neil Postman and Charles Weingartner, *Teaching as a Subversive Activity* (New York: Dell Publishing Co., 1969), p. 21.

2.   Postman and Weingartner, *Ibid.*, 1969, *ad passim* pp. 19-20.

3.   See Arthur J. Lewis, "Education for the 21st Century," *Educational Leadership*, September 1983, p. 10.

4.   See Harriet Tyson-Bernstein, *A Conspiracy of Good Intentions: America's Textbook Fiasco* (Washington, D.C.: The Council for Basic Education, 1988; and Lynne V. Cheney,

Tyrannical Machines (Washington, D.C.: The National Endowment for the Humanities, 1990).

5. See Mortimer J. Adler, *The Paideia Proposal: An Educational Manifesto* (New York: Macmillan Co., 1982), pp. 28-32 *ad passim*.

6. Grant Wiggins. "Creating a Thought-Provoking Curriculum," *American Educator*, Winter 1987, p. 11.

Three
REDEFINING
SCHOOL OUTCOMES

The school curriculum is very crucial to the kind of school we want to make. Teachers determine *how* children learn, but the curriculum determines *what* they learn. A curriculum can be viewed from two perspectives: its general characteristics and its content. General characteristics are the structural features of a curriculum -- how it is designed and implemented. Content is the substance of the curriculum -- what is to be learned from it. Let's first examine the structural characteristics of the kind of curriculum envisioned in a learning rather than teaching oriented school; then we will consider the content of the new curriculum.

The new curriculum should be designed to achieve demonstrable learning objectives. Learning objectives are statements of desired outcomes -- what we want as the end result of the educational process. The primary function of schooling is to organize the learning activities of children to ensure that all learning objectives are addressed by the end of the schooling period.

Organizing the New Curriculum

It makes sense to think of the 12 years of basic schooling as consisting of three distinct but interrelated components. I will call these components "learning levels." Learning Level I consists of the first four years of formal schooling; Learning Level II takes in the next four years; and so forth. This roughly corresponds with a primary or elementary school (Level I), middle school (Level II) and high school (Level III) configuration.

The curriculum for each learning level covers the entire four years, with intermediate steps along the way that are not necessarily in school-year or age-graded increments. Learning outcomes are developed for each four-year period with increased levels of achievement and breadth of knowledge expected as the student progresses from one level to another. The curriculum is designed so that students may work at their own pace on the specific learning objectives designated for their learning level, but they are expected to reach the *highest* level of understanding or proficiency possible for *all* learning objectives by the end of *each* learning level (or ages 9, 13 and 17).

The advantages of this organizational scheme are that it allows us to break up the curriculum into manageable units, making it easier to adapt it to natural stages of physical and mental growth. It permits us to better accommodate short-term variations in student maturation by extending the learning period beyond a single calendar year. The greatest difficulty is that it requires a much different school structure and a greater ability to plan and keep track of each student's performance than we now have.

The new curriculum has these features: (1) it identifies, defines and describes the learning outcomes applicable to each level of learning; (2) it specifies the kind of learning activities that are appropriate for children at various stages of physical, intellectual and emotional development; and (3) it identifies for the student various resources available to achieve each learning outcome, such as books, videotapes, professional journals, newspapers, magazines, literature, poetry, art, experiments, discussions and reference works.

In the early years of schooling, the curriculum focuses on the acquisition and enhancement of skills needed to learn. A major goal of the curriculum in these years is to have children take increasing responsibility for their learning. As they mature in their learning ability, the curriculum focuses more on learning ideas and concepts basic to understanding their world. However, throughout the entire schooling experience, emphasis is continually placed on development of the intellectual skills necessary for intelligent use of knowledge.

This kind of curriculum makes the learning process essentially student-driven, meaning that students in the upper levels can pursue the learning described in the curriculum on their own under the guidance of mentors who help them find the most effective way to achieve the learning objectives. The curriculum is designed so that it does not require someone to "teach" it. Unconstrained by textbooks and formal lesson plans, each student is free to pursue learning in a variety of ways. The intent is to open up the avenues of knowledge so that a student's learning is not dependent on what a teacher knows, what a textbook contains, or the motivational level of others in the class.

What Students Should Learn

Almost every study of American education has recommended a change in what is taught in our schools. In basic agreement with others who have critiqued the current curriculum, I believe a new curriculum should focus on (a) learning skills, (b) personal and social skills, and (c) the knowledge one must have to function competently in a 21st century environment.

---

a. Learning Skills

The Paideia Group regards the basic learning skills as reading, writing, speaking, listening, observing, measuring, estimating and calculating. These skills are linguistic, mathematical and scientific in nature, and include competence in the use of a wide range of symbolic devices such as calculators, computers and scientific instruments. They are skills that everyone needs to learn anything in school or elsewhere. Without them it is impossible to go on learning by one's self, whether for pleasure, to qualify for a new job, or to be promoted in the present one.[1]

In addition to acquiring a proficiency in the skills basic to learning, students need intellectual, analytical and communication skills -- the ability to set goals, cross-relate ideas, conceptualize, reason to a conclusion from a set of facts, explain clearly what they are thinking and feeling, negotiate, plan, organize and make decisions.

Putting it another way, to live in our technological, pluralistic and changing global society, graduates of our schools need the ability to bring together divergent ideas across all academic specialties, organize their thoughts, reach conclusions, and in the end use knowledge wisely. Information alone is not enough to solve problems. The ability to comprehend that information -- to analyze it, synthesize it, and apply it in a value-oriented way -- is also necessary. The ability to learn and conceptualize is as important as factual knowledge and specific skills.[2] In essence, this means the graduates of our schools must be proficient in the "survival skills" of a learning society.

b. Personal and Social Skills

Learning to learn is critical to survival, but social and behavioral skills are very important to success in almost any realm of life. We will not serve our children well unless their

---

schooling includes nurturing of those human behavior traits so important in a society of interdependent relationships -- traits such as honesty, dependability, judgment, ability to plan and make decisions, cooperation and many more. In fact, many of these very traits are necessary for success in school itself.

Much emphasis is placed today on preparing our young people to enter the world of work. However, most employers I know are at least as concerned about the personal habits and social style of their employees as about their job skills. It does a company little good to have a superbly trained technician who is often tardy, careless, undependable, quarrelsome, uncooperative, unkempt, chemically dependent or inattentive to detail. The same applies to many other life situations as well. Learning objectives devoted to nurturing valued personal and social behavior can be a natural part of the school curriculum. We only need to make them valued outcomes when the curriculum is designed.

c. Specific Items of Information and Basic Concepts

Perhaps the most vexing aspect of developing a new kind of curriculum is to determine how to lead our children through the labyrinth of information we are generating. Recent studies of American education have pointed to the need for a more holistic approach to knowledge. As knowledge grows, this proposal makes more and more sense. It is unrealistic to think we can educate our youth for a lifetime of living in 12 years of childhood schooling. They will spend the rest of their lives learning and still only know a small portion of what is knowable.

The issue is whether students are encouraged to make a broad inquiry into a wide range of intellectual issues relevant to living in the 21st century, or whether they are to spend their time learning the specific, detailed concepts and theories of various academic specialties. I believe it is better to gain familiarity with the generic substance of human knowledge than to master

---

some "academic field" during the first 12 years of formal schooling.

Students should experience the interrelatedness of ideas, the broad implications and applications of knowledge, and the process of discovery, dissemination and use of information. While learning the essential vocabulary and some basic concepts of the academic specialty known as "biology," students also should learn about such things as genetic engineering, organ transplants, sexuality, life support systems, disease transmission, nutrition, what it means to be brain dead, and physical changes in cells due to aging or substance abuse.

Understanding the Main Ideas of the Specialties

Every academic specialty has developed many concepts that have great explanatory power; concepts that enable us to organize, understand and use information from many disciplines; concepts that give us the capacity to integrate knowledge, see interrelationships and create for ourselves the "big picture." There are many such "main ideas." Let me suggest just a few of them to illustrate the value of concentrating on a select group of main ideas rather than attempting to cover in a cursory manner the mass of information that has accumulated in every academic discipline.

Let's begin with an examination of the idea of energy. The idea of energy helps us to understand physical phenomena (e.g., heat and light), industrialization (it requires electricity and steam), astronomical phenomena (radiation and solar power), natural resources (oil, coal and wood), body metabolism (blood sugar level), music and literature (movement and excitement), and economics (energy costs and availability). As we can see, thinking about energy can help us understand many seemingly discrete things that give it the desired explanatory power. Typically, students only study about energy in a physical science class because it is thought of primarily as a concept of physics.

Understood only in that context, the idea loses much of its explanatory value.

As another example, take the concept of interaction -- the effect two or more things have upon each other. The idea is basic to scientific explanations (e.g., causation and ecosystems), but it also can be found in psychology (psychedelic drugs and alcohol), economics (interest rates and business decisions), and health (fatty foods and colesterol). If we recognize the interrelatedness of things, we begin to look for interactive effects as a way to understand many things in life. Learning to think about "how this will effect that" increases our ability to think logically.

Let's examine one more concept -- rhythm. The idea of rhythm can be found in music, literature, poetry and dance, but it also can be found in physics, body functions, language and athletics. Once again, we find that the idea is not limited to a single human intellectual endeavor. Rhythm may be a problem in dance, but it also can be a problem in learning to shoot free throws in a basketball game or in the functioning of our heart.

This discussion of main ideas is important because it can resolve the concern about too much emphasis upon facts without understanding why the facts are important. One can illustrate energy in a laboratory through a routine experiment. However, energy has importance far beyond what can be learned about it in a physics lab. Energy is a fundamental element in an industrialized economy, in a well body and in international politics. Building the curriculum around main ideas would enable students to pursue multiple applications of knowledge and force thoughtful inquiry rather than rote learning of terms, definitions and facts. It would help children to think about what they are learning and to use their minds well.

Creating a New Outcome-Based Curriculum

The concerns most commonly expressed when we propose moving from the traditional content-based curriculum to one that is outcome-based are: (1) how we determine what outcomes are desired; (2) how we create an outcome-based curriculum; and (3) how we document that children have attained the expected outcomes. The first issue is one of determining what all children should reasonably be expected to know and be able to do at the various learning levels. The second issue relates to how we create a curriculum that is challenging, dynamic and flexible, and still ensures that all students attain the envisioned

> **The activities that represent the expected outcomes must be rich, challenging and meaningful to the student.**

outcomes. The third issue is one of devising valid ways by which children can demonstrate what they have learned.

As for determining the desired outcomes, the initial task is to establish a process for developing a public consensus on what young people are expected to know and be able to do after 12 years of formal schooling. Connecticut, Maine, Utah and Kentucky have recently developed goals and objectives that describe in general terms the competencies desired in the graduates of their public schools. These goals and objectives constitute the common core of learning on which the education system is to be based.

The process for developing educational goals can take many forms. Each of the states just mentioned used a somewhat different methodology. In Kentucky, the goals were initially developed by a Council on School Performance Standards appointed by Governor Wilkinson early in 1989. They were subsequently made part of the Education Reform Act of 1990 after legislative hearings demonstrated they had broad public support.[3] By whatever means educational goals are derived, they must be clearly stated and have broad public support.

Creating an outcome-based curriculum of the type described here is a technical process that must involve broad participation by educators. Teachers must create a "crosswalk" from the present curriculum to the new one. The first step involves identifying the skills and main ideas that are most important for students to learn if they are to attain the goals set for the education system. The product is a matrix of skills (learning, personal and social) and main ideas grouped according to their appropriate level of learning.

The next step is to create activities which, if performed correctly, would demonstrate proficiency in a skill or an appropriate understanding of a main idea. The specific skill(s) or main idea(s) to be demonstrated are designated for each activity so that both teacher and student know what is to be learned from it. Different activities may be required to initially learn a skill or to understand an idea than would be used to gain proficiency in their use.

The activities that represent the expected outcomes must be rich, challenging, and meaningful to the student. Each group of activities should become increasingly more complex and require an expanding application of knowledge and skills as the student progresses through the various levels of learning. Prototype activities should be developed by the state to provide uniform levels of comprehensiveness and difficulty statewide. However, teachers would be expected to develop and use activities of their own that emulate the state prototypes. These school-based activities should provide students the same learning experience as if they had performed the prototype activities. All of these activities in the aggregate make up the "curriculum." They represent everything students are expected to know and do.

The final step is to establish levels of proficiency for each activity that reflect varying degrees of expertise. Such standards then become the basis on which to document how well students have learned what we expect them to know and be able to do at each learning level. Expert, intermediate or novice performance might be examples of levels of proficiency. Acceptable ' performance should be at least at the intermediate level. Of course, other terminology and more gradients could be used where more appropriate.

Monitoring and Reporting Student Learning

In most schools today tests are given at appointed times, graded by the teacher and reported back to the students shortly after each test. An aggregate "grade" is assigned at the end of a school term to reflect the overall level of learning achieved. The assessment of learning is quite different in the kind of school we envision here. The tests that now come in finals week will come at the end of projects or upon completion of specific learning objectives. The demonstration of learning is integrated across more than a single objective in most cases.

Statistical norming is unnecessary because all students are expected to perform at or above the acceptable proficiency level. There is no average or mean "score" for the class. The only meaningful statistic is the percentage of students who attain the various levels of proficiency. The curriculum is divided into small units built around groups of learning activities and objectives. Certain tasks are specifically designed to assess each student's level of achievement on various learning objectives. Students may be assessed as groups or as individuals, depending on the nature of the tasks that make up the activity. Students regularly demonstrate their knowledge and skills through their learning activities.

The learning feedback received by each student is twofold. First, students are expected to assess their own performance against the performance modeled in the state-developed prototype. Since students as well as teachers know the kind of performance required for each level of proficiency, they are able to gauge their own progress. Second, teachers regularly observe and validate the student's own assessment to ensure correct self-evaluation. In this manner students can gain a realistic understanding of their own performance and uniform standards of performance for all students can be enforced. The continuous feedback process gives both students and teachers a continuing awareness of the need for improvement in a timely fashion.

How We Can Get There From Here

Implementing a curriculum that is so different from what now exists requires redesigning the approach to teaching and learning that has characterized American education for more than a century. This is not just raising standards or creating new courses for students to take. A whole new way of schooling is being created.

Since the teaching profession will be profoundly affected, their participation in the change is critical to its success. The professional identity of teachers, including their legal certification, is directly related to and manifested in the curriculum. "I am an English teacher," we hear someone say, which is different from saying "I teach English." In many ways the former more accurately represents the person than the latter. The thought of eliminating or changing courses strikes terror in the hearts of teachers, for in that single action they may lose their whole professional identity. If there are no English courses, what becomes of an "English teacher"?

One key to minimizing this problem is to involve teachers in the development of the new curriculum. Another is more subtle and involves getting them to understand that abolishing courses does not mean abolishing teachers. As their role changes in the classroom, hopefully they can come to think of themselves as "mentors in English" rather than as English teachers.

Parents also will find this approach totally unfamiliar and may fear that their children will not learn what they learned in school. Although many people say they want a better education for their children, the prospect of significantly changing the way schools operate can be very disconcerting. In this case we are asking people to support considerable change in something that has changed very little in their lifetime. Parental resistance can be formidable if parents do not understand why the changes are being made and how they will know what their children are learning.

One point of great concern to parents is knowing how well their children are doing on an "age-graded" basis, since this is the primary indicator of academic progress in the present system. It is very important that the results of the continuous assessment process be reported regularly to parents. They will need help in understanding the progress their child is making toward the expected outcomes at the 4th, 8th and 12th grade level. Unless teachers can clearly document this progress at regular intervals and parents can feel comfortable with this documentation, parents will push to go back to age-graded report cards. Although progression in learning is more relevant information than an end-of-year grade, parents want assurance that their children are doing well and progressing satisfactorily in relation to their age peers.

Another concern parents will express is their inability to know how much math or science a child is learning if he or she is not taking a specific "course" in math and science. Interdiscipli-nary learning is superior to isolated specialty courses because children gain through it a much broader understanding and use of the information they learn. However, reports on student achievement must enable parents to see that their children can do everything they expect them to do. The "back to basics" movement a decade ago came about in large part because parents discovered their children could not do simple arithmetic or read simple instructions. Certainly this concern will remain. Reports given to parents about what children know and can do must clearly demonstrate that they can do the basics and much more.

The ability of children to perform well on certain college entrance examinations also will concern some parents. They want assurance that this new curriculum will not lower their children's test scores. The role such tests should play in college admission decisions has been debated for many years, but the reality is that they are still used. It should be noted in this regard that the vendors of these tests are currently revising them to make them more performance-based, so these tests may become more like those proposed here in the near future. In any event, schools will need to be aware of how their students are doing on these examinations.

High school transcripts also have been used for college admission purposes. Colleges and universities expect entering students to have received a passing grade in certain academic subjects. The curriculum described here is not organized around the traditional academic specialties on which college curricula are built. Therefore, college admissions officials will need help to reconcile their "Carnegie unit" system to the new curriculum in the K-12 education system.

Although these concerns about meeting college entrance requirements are important, the public secondary schools must do more than prepare children for entrance to college in the traditional sense. We cannot continue to view our secondary schools as a "college prep" system. All children must be prepared to learn and to succeed in postsecondary educational programs. However, it must be recognized that a secondary education is now part of the universal education system.

On a more general note, none of what has been described here is entirely new or untried. A curriculum based on learning objectives is decades old. What *is* new is changing the objectives from "covering material" in textbooks to demonstrating learning that reflects broad outcomes. In the next chapter I will discuss how children will learn the new curriculum and how this will change the roles of teachers and others.

Notes for Chapter Three

1. Taken *ad passim* from Adler, Mortimer J. *The Paideia Proposal: An Educational Manifesto* (New York: Macmillan Co., 1982), pp. 25-27.

2. See Ernest L. Boyer. *High School: A Report on Secondary Education in America* (New York: Harper & Row, 1983), p. 117; Arthur J. Lewis, "Education for the 21st Century," *Education Leadership*, September 1983, p. 10; and National Association of State Boards of Education, "Thinking Strategically about the Future," *Education Week*, November 14, 1984, p. 19.

3. See The Report of the Council on School Performance Standards, *Preparing Kentucky Youth for the Next Century: What Students Should Know and Be Able to Do and How Learning Should be Assessed*. (Frankfort, KY: The Education and Humanities Cabinet, September 1989); and Section I of House Bill 940 enacted in the 1990 session of the Kentucky General Assembly.

Four
A SCHOOL
FOR LEARNING

If teachers don't "teach," then how will students learn? Perhaps the best way to answer this question is to draw a word picture of what a school designed for learning might look like. First I will describe such a school in conceptual terms. Then we will "visit" a prototype school to illustrate the concepts I have described in abstract terms. The purpose of this chapter is to create an ideograph (or mental picture) of what a school designed for learning might be like.

The basic premise of a school is to provide a learning rather than a teaching environment for students. Students organize their work to achieve specific learning outcomes. Each day they engage in a variety of learning activities designed to help them achieve these outcomes. The learning activities will vary according to each child's level of educational, physical and emotional development. The selection and assessment of learning activities is guided by professionals I will refer to as "mentors."

I have chosen the word "mentor" advisedly. Names given to us tend to define what we do. Greek in origin, the word mentor was ascribed to a friend of Odysseus entrusted with the

---

education of his son. The name "teacher" implies a person instructing others about something. A mentor is a trusted counselor or guide; a tutor and coach. The word mentor best expresses what I see as the role of a teacher in a school designed for learning.

Generally, students are expected to pursue their learning activities on their own under the supervision of a mentor or a paraprofessional I will call a "learning assistant." Mentors and learning assistants help students locate relevant materials, conduct experiments, understand what they are reading, direct discussions, provoke questions, challenge ideas and generally stimulate and guide the student's learning process. The role of the student is to achieve the learning outcomes of the curriculum, turning to the mentor or learning assistant for help as the need arises.

Students will often be working on multiple learning outcomes through a single learning activity. For example, they might undertake a task that focuses simultaneously on achieving outcomes relating to communication, grammar, promptness, neatness, inferential thinking, data collection and group dynamics. Such an approach offers an economy of effort for both students and teachers.

Throughout the entire schooling experience, there is continual emphasis placed on development of higher order intellectual skills such as the ability to bring together divergent ideas, organize thoughts, reason to conclusions from a set of facts, explain clearly what one thinks and feels, and to use knowledge wisely.[1] Students are encouraged and allowed to learn as much as time permits, unconstrained by the abilities of others or by course content.

Students may meet in classrooms as they do now, but not necessarily to receive "instruction." Many classrooms will be organized around student workstations equipped for various types of learning activities. Students will work at the place most appropriate for the learning activities they are undertaking at the time. Also, they may be working individually or in groups depending on the nature of the learning activity.

In the early years of schooling, small children are not yet able to direct their own learning, so mentors guide them through experiences that help them acquire and enhance the skills needed to learn (e.g., reading, writing, speaking, listening, computing, etc.), using such methodologies as computer-based instruction, group reading and the like. A major goal of schooling in the early years is to have children take increasing responsibility for directing their own learning activities. The intent is to develop self-sufficient "learners" -- children able to take charge of their own learning now and later on as adults. As children mature in their learning ability, the role of the mentor gradually shifts to one of providing personal guidance, understanding, encouragement and coaching to the student.

A Visit to a School Designed for Learning

Imagine arriving at school early Monday morning about the tenth week into the term. We are visiting a middle school -- Level II in our three-level curriculum (roughly equivalent to fifth through eighth grades). Classes will begin in about 15 minutes. The mentors, curriculum specialists, learning assistants, and learning diagnosticians are in their weekly meeting together. Today they are discussing various problems some mentors have encountered in getting access for their students to the videotape equipment; hearing an explanation of some new learning activities that will be pre-tested by certain mentors this week; and learning about some changes in certain learning activities now in use that were suggested by two mentors about a month ago.

The meeting breaks up and they all go to their respective work area. As we make our way to the first classroom we will

---

visit, the school coordinator (formerly the school principal) explains that each classroom is supervised by one or more learning assistants. She points out that learning assistants keep children on task, help them organize their work, oversee some types of learning activities, keep certain administrative records, and generally oversee the learning activities of the children in their care.

Students already are gathering in the room. It is casual but orderly. Chairs are arranged in small groups of four or five each. The learning assistants share a desk in the corner, inconspicuous among bookshelves and work tables placed around the room. The first order of business on this particular Monday is to help students prepare work plans for the next two weeks. As we take our places at the back of the room, the learning assistant gets the attention of the students and explains briefly the learning outcomes they are expected to focus on over the next few days.

One of the mentors is in the classroom with us. Her name is Marsha. She has been with this group of students for two years. They are now entering their third together. Most of the students are 12 years old, but some are younger or older than that. Marsha understands how important it is for children to have confidence in and feel close to their mentor. She also is secure enough in her own ability that she is not offended when she realizes that a particular student and she just don't "hit it off." When this first happens, another mentor will try to work with the student, but sometimes this doesn't work either. Occasionally, the problems are with the students themselves. Marsha comments that, with the help of a counselor, several of her students were eventually reassigned to other mentors. In return, Marsha got several new students.

Mentors and learning assistants typically work as a team. Sometimes as many as three or four mentors will be assigned to a cluster of students in order to provide the breadth of knowledge required for the learning activities they are involved in at the time. Today, the mentor and learning assistants are encouraging students to work in small groups, since one of the learning outcomes at this level is improvement of teamwork skills. Students are moving about the room as they try to find others who are working on the same learning activities. As they discuss among themselves how they might go about their work, the mentor and learning assistant move from group to group answering questions, giving guidance and generally making sure that the students are properly focusing their efforts.

The general focus at this time is on energy. In earlier units they studied its historic and technological importance. At a future time they will examine the physical properties of energy and its presence in nonphysical forms such as in literature and music. At the present time, they are examining the economic aspects of energy. Among the learning activities they may pursue at this time are an examination of:

1. OPEC: its history, composition, organization, power and economic influence on the U.S. and other nations.

2. Nuclear Power: its history, current applications, cost of production relative to other competing energy sources, environmental concerns, costs associated with disposition of high-level radiation waste, safety and its economic role in a petroleum oriented nation.

3. Petroleum: national and world reserves, the cost of alternative methods of drilling, geological and other environmental consequences of drilling, the economic importance of derivatives of petroleum, sources of oil consumed in the U.S., the pricing of oil, cost of exploration, and the economic future of the petroleum industry.

---

4. National Energy Policy: the history of U.S. policies regarding various forms of energy, regulation of the energy industry, conservation, research and development of alternative sources of energy, impact of government policy on exploration of oil, gas and coal, the use of oil as an economic sanction, and the consequences of being an oil-dependent nation.

5. Conservation: what is being done at the state, community, school and home level to conserve energy.

Students are allowed to expand upon the subtopics and need not address every one of them. However, everyone in the class will learn something about all five economic aspects of energy.

About 15 minutes into the discussion, Marsha breaks in to make certain everyone understands the specific learning outcomes for this unit, i.e., understanding the idea of energy in the context of economics, improving literature research skills, expository writing, documentation of findings, teamwork, proper allocation of time, meeting a deadline, and oral presentation of key findings. The students will be evaluated on all of these outcomes through this particular learning activity. The task of planning their work with multiple outcomes in mind is not new to them. It is done regularly, about every two or three weeks.

As the plans are completed, the mentor reads them, suggests any modifications needed to make them acceptable, and approves them after appropriate revisions are made. (Only mentors are permitted to approve learning plans.) These students now have a "learning contract" with the mentor and are expected to perform everything included in their work plans. The mentor examines these plans very carefully to ensure that they have proper breadth, require a reasonable level of effort to complete, and address all of the learning outcomes.

We now move on to another classroom down the hall where we find students arranged in several concentric circles, some sitting on the floor and others in chairs behind them. Three students are engaged in a heated debate over the issue of withdrawing life support systems from persons declared brain dead. Each of the three has written a paper on the medical, psychological, legal and ethical aspects of the issue. These papers were distributed to the other students the previous day. This learning activity requires each student to take a position and defend it based on information they gathered from these written papers. A fourth student moderates the debate, directing questions from the students gathered in front of the debaters.

Shortly after we get comfortable and begin to feel the intensity of the discussion, one of the learning assistants calls "time out." He now asks each of the debaters to take a different side of the issue from the one just defended. It's obvious that some find this a bit difficult, but they knew this would be expected of them so they are prepared. Fifteen minutes later, the learning assistant breaks in again and asks for a volunteer to cross-examine each of the three debaters, five minutes for each one, pursuing only one line of questioning with each one. Jacob quickly raises his hand, but the learning assistant reminds him that he had done this the last time. It's time for another student to try it.

It is obvious that these students are not just learning about the issue under discussion; they also are learning behavioral and intellectual skills such as how to reason, defend one's position articulately and with rationality, see arguments from both sides of an issue, and "take the heat" of direct examination without getting hostile or losing poise. All are very useful skills and behaviors to be developed while learning a great deal about a significant medical, social and ethical issue.

This particular learning activity is being videotaped by the learning assistant. Later in the day, a communications mentor

---

and debate coach will view the videotape and arrange a meeting with the debators to discuss their performance. Prior to that time, however, the debaters will view the tape together and critique their own performance and offer suggestions to each other. It is important that students first evaluate their own work because the mentor will ask them to point out what they saw as the strengths and weaknesses of their performance. Such self-assessment is required for all learning activities. Students are always expected to assess the quality of their work.

The session is now ended and chairs scrape on the floor as students begin to move about, finding a spot where they can continue to work. The debaters have gone to another room to view the videotape and critique their performance. When they meet with their mentor they will again go over some of the skills or behaviors she thinks they need to improve when preparing for their next debate a month from now. The mentor also will confirm the student's own assessment, correcting it if necessary by pointing out things overlooked or incorrectly evaluated. Over time the mentor will work with all of the students in this group. Each one will be personally coached to continually enhance his or her skills in rational argument.

Shortly after the students have rearranged the room for personal study, Rosemarie asks one of the learning assistants for permission to go to her workstation to view a videotape she has gotten from a local social agency that explains the procedures involved in placing children for adoption. She learned about the tape while explaining to a relative that her class was studying changing patterns in family life. If the videotape appeals to her, she would like to show it to interested students in the class. She also informs her mentor that she has finalized arrangements for her family attorney to make a presentation to the class on Thursday on the legal responsibilities of parenthood, something she had committed herself to in her work plan.

I mentioned that Rosemarie was going to her workstation. Throughout the school there are personal workstations shared by students that are equipped with computers and other technology with which to perform many of the learning activities. Some workstations are equipped with video capability allowing students to examine visual and written material stored on videotape or laser discs. Students also can watch instructional programming available by satellite at scheduled times during the day.

These workstations are very versatile. Students use them to locate information and perform many learning activities required by the curriculum. Essays, mathematical and scientific problems, musical compositions, graphics and many other things are done on computers. Mentors can follow the progress of their students by calling up their computer work files for examination. They can assess their students' work and even leave instructions for them from their own workstation.

As Rosemarie leaves for her workstation, Gomez checks out a portable computer to use at home tonight. He wants to type a portion of a report on genetic transmission of disease that he and two other students are working on together. Several other students moved their chairs together and asked the learning assistant to sit in as they discuss how to organize a skit they want to give titled "Rights, Privileges and Responsibilities in the Use of a Telephone." The topic is one they thought up in response to this learning objective: "Improve communication within the family on a matter of personal importance."

I will end the vignette at this point. Obviously, the activities described here would not be applicable to all age groups. Other topics or learning outcomes might have been used. It is not material to the concerns of this book whether the people who carry the burden for guiding student learning are called mentors, career professionals, master teachers or lead teachers. The key issue is what they do. Whatever their title, and however they may be professionally "differentiated," little progress will be made in changing what is fundamentally wrong with the American approach to education if we still make them responsible for transmitting information in classes organized around subjects and textbooks in age-graded classrooms. In any case, I trust this description of a school designed for learning creates a mental picture of what schooling might be like if we changed the roles of students and teachers and significantly altered our general approach to education.

Notes to Chapter Four

1.   See Ernest L. Boyer, *High School: A Report on Secondary Education in America* (New York: Harper & Row, 1983), p. 117.

Five
CREATING
NEW SCHOOLS

A school designed for learning is clearly a different place than teachers and students now experience. The roles of both are significantly altered. The new school requires people with special skills not now prevalent in the education work force. How must the teaching profession be changed in order to bring about the kind of changes we want for students? How is a learning-oriented school to be structured and staffed? How can these changes occur? This chapter is devoted to a discussion of these and related issues.

Creating a New Vision of Schools

In many respects, our present schools are like industrial job shops in which individual workers ply their craft in relative isolation from one another. The typical American classroom is a self-contained subsystem -- a "microcosm school" as it were. The classroom is an isolated workplace. The teacher works alone to perform all tasks associated with a teacher's main function -- imparting knowledge to students. Typically, teachers prepare their own lesson plans, prepare and grade their own examinations, evaluate each student's progress, identify and diagnose any learning problems and prescribe their remedies.

Not only is such an approach to schooling pedagogically unsound, it also is inefficient. The system is internally redundant, each teacher being required to replicate the work of others without benefit of cooperation or teamwork. Larger school systems often are able to augment the teacher's work with various support services, some of which are highly specialized. Even in these schools, however, the nature of the classroom remains essentially the same.

The situation just described is inherent in a teacher-based method of education -- the very foundation on which the American education system is built. It hardly could be otherwise. What goes on in the classroom is organized to facilitate teaching, and student learning is teacher dependent. It should be clear by now that what teachers presently are required to do is almost antithetical to what we might expect in a school designed for learning.

National Recognition of a Need for Change

In 1986, the Carnegie Task Force on Teaching as a Profession acknowledged the need to change the focus of the classroom from teaching to learning -- from the passive acquisition of facts and routines to the active application of ideas to problems. The Task Force believed three challenges had to be met at once if we are to obtain and retain teachers of high intellectual ability. One of these is to "redesign" the school structure.[1] The Holmes Group, a consortium of education deans and academic administrators from about 40 research universities, subsequently proposed significant changes in the way teachers are prepared for their profession.[2] The Holmes Group also concluded that improving teacher education required parallel changes in a school structure that it characterized as anachronistic and archaic.

The Holmes Group and the Carnegie Task Force both stress the need to redefine what teachers do, but their solutions are framed to fit a teacher-based classroom -- the historical approach to schooling in America. Both groups advocated the creation of different levels of teacher but left relatively unchanged the basic educational structure -- a teaching and teacher-dependent approach to learning. If we are to have the kind of school we need, the redefinition of what teachers do in schools should be grounded in a much different philosophy of how schools and their work force are to function.

Practicing the Education Profession

In a profession, the practitioner operates from a research and practice knowledge base. Judgments about clients are made according to their unique needs or circumstances. The practitioner has available all the materials and equipment needed to help a client and uses his or her expertise to guide a client to a desired outcome. The practitioner monitors a client's progress and makes corrections in the prescribed action as circumstances require. Practitioners often specialize and will work in concert with other specialists or professionals when a client's needs go beyond the scope of their specialty.

In the case of professional educators (or mentors), there is a body of knowledge and practice about how children develop and learn. They also have expertise in certain knowledge domains that enables them to uniquely help children learn certain skills and understand the ideas they are to master. The professional educator is able to monitor the progress of the student and take whatever steps are necessary to ensure the learner progresses as expected. In a certain sense, a school is like a "group practice" of education specialists who work together with all students to help them master all the learning objectives set for them.

The professional responsibilities of teachers will significantly change when students are made more responsible for their own learning. In a learner-based system they will observe, assess and coach students; keep records on their progress; confer with other professionals; prepare new instructional materials for student use; evaluate the learning activities they are using and create new ones when appropriate; and keep current on child development and other relevant research.

Teachers may contend they are doing most of these things now, but the real change will come in their work style. Teachers will no longer be classroom-bound. They may move from room to room to observe and coach students. Many student learning activities will have multiple objectives, so more than one teacher can observe, assess and coach the same student

---

The professional responsibilities of teachers will significantly change when students are made more responsible for their own learning.

---

at the same time on the same activity. In fact, many of the observations and assessments of performance can be done at a computer workstation or by televideo. Since continuous direct contact with students is no longer part of a teacher's function, time is available to confer with other professionals, update student performance records, and engage in professional development activities.

Obviously, this means that students also are doing things differently. Paraprofessionals, whom I have called "learning assistants," provide the daily oversight of students and perform most of the administrative tasks now performed by teachers. They make certain that students are present and orderly, remain on task, and are progressing satisfactorily on their learning objectives. When something is amiss with a student, the learning assistant reports this to the appropriate professional.

The staffing configuration of a school can now change. Teachers can be employed for a full year since some of their work doesn't require the presence of students. They are not bound by the student time schedule, so they can organize their own workday as any other professional does. Teachers will gain real control over their time and how it is used.

Creating a Professional Practice School

The typical school today tends to be a bureaucratic organization in which work is standardized and routine. Teachers are primarily rewarded for doing their work according to the rules rather than for the quality of the outcome. A new educational system must be devised that is based on a professional practice model rather than a production or bureaucratic model. Teachers (or mentors) should be able to guide the learning process based on a professional assessment of individual learning needs and selection of the most appropriate learning strategy for each child.

A new educational system must be devised that is based on a professional practice model rather than a production or bureaucratic model.

In the present school structure, most instructional decisions are made outside the local school. Students are distributed almost at random, in many cases by computer program, according to subject specialty such as a learning skill (reading, writing, etc.) or academic discipline (social studies, science, mathematics, etc.) and in some instances even according to perceived "ability" levels. Teachers are limited to the students assigned to them with no regard for compatibility.

Time and materials are a critical resource for a professional. Teachers in the present school structure have little or no control over either one of these elements. Textbooks, which are the center of the traditional curriculum, often are selected (as in Kentucky) by a state-level selection commission. Even student time on task is determined by rigid daily time schedules. Children move from subject to subject and sometimes from teacher to teacher on an hourly basis without regard to what they may have been doing at the time. Even the teacher's own schedule often is determined by a central office computer.

Educators rightly point out that the individualized approach to schooling envisioned here is very difficult to implement within the present structure of schools. Teachers cannot create a school environment that meets the unique learning needs of children unless they have control over the selection of instructional methods and materials and of the use of teacher and student time, building space and other school resources. Most of these decisions are presently made by central authorities in the system and not by the people closest to the student.

Education professionals at the school level are in the best position to assess the educational needs of children and to design the most appropriate learning program for them. Moving instructional decisions to the school site is a first step in the creation of a professional practice school. The second step is to create a process through which teachers and others can make these decisions. In the terminology of the day this is called "on-site decision making."

Moving responsibility for instructional decisions to the school site is not an issue of governance or power. It is a matter of providing educators the right to make professional decisions that directly affect student learning. These decisions would include at least the following: selection of instructional materials; allocation of teacher and student time; the scheduling of student assessments; utilization of school space; allocation of teacher time; use of paraprofessionals and other school personnel; and the school site budget. It also is highly desirable that school site staff be involved in decisions about hiring teachers and staff.

Since many instructional decisions are professional in nature, they should be made by the individual teacher on a case-by-case basis. However, other matters such as the purchase of technology and learning materials, assignment of students to mentors, and the use of building space all affect the school staff collectively. Therefore, there must be a process in place by which to resolve matters such as these. Some kind of on-site "school council" should be created for this purpose. Decisions of the council will need the support of the whole school staff, so council members ought to be representative of the various interests within the school.[3]

The intent of having a school council is to facilitate discussion and consensus, not to create another level of bureaucracy. Professional collegiality has been a missing ingredient in schools for many years. School councils provide a mechanism for involving the stakeholders in decisions that affect their professional practice. If some matter has to be decided by a narrow majority vote, then consensus doesn't exist and the issue most likely remains unresolved. School councils and the decision processes they create should promote meaningful discussion about how best to organize their professional workplace.

One might question the wisdom of trying to manage a school by committee. The situation is somewhat analagous to the medical profession. The hospital is managed by a hospital administrator but the medical staff makes all the clinical decisions about patient treatment. Teachers should make those decisions that directly affect their capacity to work effectively with students; on the other hand, professional educators should not be involved in general management decisions that can be left either to the central office or to a school-site administrator. Such things as bus scheduling, building maintenance, security, food service and cleaning are very important to the overall school environment, but they are generally beyond the scope of an educator's expertise.

On-site decision making will change the role of school principals. In the American school, principals are a mixture of educator and administrator, but mostly they are administrators. Research on "effective schools" indicates that students generally perform better when a principal is an "instructional leader." However, the pressures of day-to-day management of schools have kept most principals occupied, with little time for instructional matters. The principal could be a member of the school council, which makes instructional decisions, as is the case in Kentucky. Whether a member of the council or not, the actual role the principal plays will depend on how each principal chooses to define it. One thing for certain, an on-site decision making process makes bureaucratic "top-down" instructional decisions totally inappropriate.

Changing Roles for Others

Moving instructional decisions to the school site also changes the roles of many central office staffs. For example, the district office will set school attendance boundaries, but teachers at the school site will determine who will work with the students assigned to the school. Some specialists in the central office, such as school counselors, pupil personnel administrators, admission officers and curriculum supervisors may remain, but how they relate to the schools in the local district will change. The functions of these people have to be integrated with the

---

Tradition may be the greatest obstacle teachers and administrators will encounter in this entire process.

---

decisions of the on-site school council and teachers. Many administrative functions like transportation and bus routing, building maintenance, food service, purchasing of equipment and materials, and a myriad of other similar functions will remain with the central office. People who perform these functions probably will see little change in their responsibilities.

Most of what teachers now do is not required by state law or regulation. Except for certification and licensure, almost everything teachers currently do is rooted in decades of tradition. Tradition may be the greatest obstacle teachers and administrators will encounter in this entire process. Changing a top-down bureaucratic organization into one based on professional practice involves changing longstanding patterns of decision-making, resource allocation and work.

Teachers and school-site personnel must be given many decisions heretofore reserved for others. Such a reallocation of decision making authority will not come easy for school administrators and other central office staff. Likewise, after many years of functioning as education "technicians" and bureaucrats, making professional judgments about the learning behavior of students and the best use of school resources will be an unfamiliar responsibility for many teachers.

Equipping a Learning-Oriented School

The nature of work has been dramatically transformed through technology -- primarily through the invention of the microprocessor. Computer technology efficiently performs in seconds many otherwise time-consuming and labor-intensive tasks. Technology also provides direct and rapid access to vast amounts of print, audio and visual information. School staffs can benefit from such technology if they learn to use it effectively.

In the past, teachers have used technology primarily to augment teaching. It was only regarded as an aid to instruction. Multimedia now enable teachers to prepare customized instructional materials for direct use by students. It also can be a productivity tool used to maintain student performance and administrative records and to assess student work performed on computers. Technology now enables student information to electronically follow students as they move from one school to another. Mentors, learning assistants and other school professionals need access to workstations where, among other things, they can record and monitor information about each student's academic progress. These workstations will have telephones and computers linked to a student information data base and equipped with software for writing and record keeping.

Each school will have a computerized Student Information System (SIS) that is programmed to maintain a progress record for every student. A mentor can generate this information any time it is needed or is requested by a parent. Periodic "report cards" for parents also will be prepared from this data base. When students who normally perform well exhibit difficulty with a particular curricular unit, the SIS can be used to evaluate the effectiveness of the learning activities that make up that unit. All information will be safeguarded through an internal security system to prevent unauthorized access to confidential student information.

Technology is rapidly advancing. As new equipment or applications emerge, mentors should be able to experiment with their use in a classroom setting. The development of new instructional uses of existing and emerging technology needs to be continually encouraged. Special facilities are needed at strategic locations to provide an opportunity for curriculum development activities and training with a wide variety of technologies.

A school in which students are in more direct control of their learning also requires that students have access to the technological tools for learning and work. The object is more than making them "computer literate." Students need to use technology for the same purposes they will use it in the adult world -- to enhance their productivity. Students should use computers to acquire information and to perform many of their learning activities. They will be expected to use computers with the same ease they would use pencil and paper technology.

When direct instruction is required, it should be delivered by technology whenever practical. Students can interact with the technology on their own schedule, which negates the need to meet together in classes. The student can go over the material as often as necessary according to personal need. Technology permits flexibility for the student, but it also ensures a consistently high-quality presentation of the material to be learned.

Located throughout the school will be personal workstations shared by students and equipped with appropriate hardware and software technology. Some workstations can be equipped with video capability for viewing visual and written material stored on videotape or laser discs. Instructional programming available by satellite can be received at these workstations at scheduled times during the day. Other workstations are computer-based for use in locating information, telecommunicating and performing many learning activities required by the curriculum. Essays, mathematical and scientific problems, musical compositions, graphics and many other things can be done by students on computers.

Technology is costly and its deployment must be wisely managed. Use of technology doesn't necessarily displace personnel or reduce costs. Much of the productivity gain achieved through automation is dedicated to expanding the amount of work we can do in the same hour. We also need to realize that both school staff and students need to learn how to properly and productively use technology or it will be misused or unused. Proper training in the use of technology is as critical to its successful use in schools as anywhere else.

Other Staff in a Learning-Oriented School

In addition to mentors and learning assistants, schools need "learning diagnosticians" trained to identify physical learning problems and their appropriate treatment. Learning diagnosticians have extensive knowledge of such topics as brain development chemistry, learning environment alternatives, cognitive and psychosomatic evaluation, and affective development.[4] Student progress is assessed regularly to identify learning problems as they arise so that a troubled student can be quickly restored to an acceptable level of progress. If a serious learning problem is found, the learning diagnostician and the student's mentors work together to develop a program of intervention and assistance to ameliorate the problem before the child's learning progress falls so far behind that extraordinary effort is required to catch up.

When a learning problem stems primarily from personal or family circumstances, school personnel should have direct access to external human services to help the child. Creation of collaborative working relationships with existing human services agencies is an essential element in the support system for schools. "Resource integrators" working at each school can ensure case collaboration between school personnel and the staffs of the various human service agencies. The resource integrators link the resources of the school with available community services to bring about a holistic approach to a child's academic and personal needs. Such people are trained in diagnostic and evaluation techniques and work on a daily basis with students and their mentors to help the school adapt to each student's personal needs.

Under the leadership of Governor Wilkinson, the Kentucky Cabinet for Human Resources and Kentucky Department of Education established in 1988 the Kentucky Integrated Delivery System (KIDS), which was piloted in 15 school districts. The Kentucky Education Reform Act of 1990 subsequently created Family Resource Centers and Youth Services Centers to be located at or near every school having more than 20 percent "at risk" students. These centers will perform the service integration function described here.

Other professionals will assume new roles. For example, curriculum supervisors will emerge as specialists in the development and refinement of learning activities that meet the unique cultural, ethnic and other special needs of children on a school-by-school basis. Counselors might be assigned to the family and youth services centers or they could be retrained to be resource integrators.

Technology coordinators will be needed to provide training and promote the development of new uses of instructional hardware and software. Personnel also will be needed to service and maintain this technology. Librarians and media specialists will work as a team with technology coordinators and mentors to develop and revise student instructional materials and provide student access to the vast information resources available within and outside the school.

Obviously, there are many acceptable ways to accomplish that end. The key point is that children should enter school to learn -- something they will be encouraged to do on their own under the tutelage of highly skilled mentors capable of helping them master whatever they are attempting to learn. Behind every mentor is a support system that ensures each child will progress academically to the best of his or her ability.

Preparing Educators for the Transition

Teachers who become mentors need the same academic background in their specialty as before. The difference is not in knowledge expertise but in how it is used to help students learn. Most teachers do not have enough training in outcome-based instruction, performance assessment, the use of technology, leadership and group decision-making skills, child and adolescent development, learning theory and research. School administrators, particularly principals, need additional training to work in the new environment.

In the prior discussion I mentioned several new positions such as learning assistants, learning diagnosticians, human resource integrators, technology coordinators and service personnel. In some instances these are only changing functions of existing personnel, but in others these are new positions presently not found in schools. In the short run, school districts will need to use personnel in the existing work force to the fullest extent possible. The present school staff should be given a reasonable opportunity to acquire the knowledge and skills required for these new positions. I believe most of them can be expected to do so successfully.

It will not be sufficient to create learning objectives and activities for students, place technology in schools, and tell everyone to get back to work. Much time, effort and money will be expended helping the work force acquire the knowledge, skills and habits of work needed in the redesigned school.

It is quite likely that the new role for teachers and the use of learning assistants could result in a substantial realignment of school staff. Some schools may want to put mentors and other professional staff on 11 month contracts, leaving only learning assistants on 9 month contracts. In this kind of environment, schools also need maximum flexibility in the reallocation of available funds. Some states reimburse schools on the basis of teacher units or teacher-to-student ratios. Schools in these states need protection from any unintended loss in funding that might result from a reduction in the number of "teaching" positions.

School accreditation standards and state laws or regulations that require certain staffing configurations also could be a problem. For example, many states have a statutory maximum teacher-student ratio that is based on the current concept of what teachers do. The intent of these laws is to keep class sizes low in the belief that children learn better in smaller classes. Would the presence of learning assistants satisfy the intent of such laws? These and similar matters need to be clarified so that the new schools do not run into accreditation problems, at least insofar as state law and regulation are concerned.

Underlying all this discussion is a presumption that extensive staff development and retraining are inherent in the transition. It will not be sufficient to create learning objectives and activities for students, place technology in schools, and tell everyone to get back to work. Much time, effort and money will be expended helping the work force acquire the knowledge, skills and habits of work needed in the redesigned school.

Almost every segment of our economy is undergoing structural changes that dramatically alter the nature of work. Business and industry invest billions of dollars annually to retrain their employees for the new work environment. Restructuring has now reached the schoolhouse and a similar investment has to be made to prepare the school employees for the transition. State policymakers should take the same position as their private sector counterparts and make the necessary human investment.

State departments of education have a major responsibility for the staff development needed for this transition. The change in philosophy is profound and its understanding cannot be left to chance. A strong program of professional development has to be devised that can reach every teacher and administrator in a very short time frame. Observing others is a very powerful way to learn, so establishing demonstration sites can be one strategy. Just as students are expected to learn on their own with the help of a mentor, teachers and other professionals can acquire the knowledge and skills they need through similar means. Technology also can be effectively used for this purpose. The state has a significant role to play in preparing mentors and developing appropriate learning activities for teachers and others to use.

Professional Qualifications and Certification

New staff configurations always raise questions about the credentials required for these positions and who should determine what they ought to be. Caution should be exercised in the creation of new titles and certification requirements for these jobs. Changes in certification also require concomitant changes in teacher college curricula. Some reasonable period of time should elapse before any new positions are formally created for certification purposes. Beyond these practical considerations, one must address the question of the value of credentials and licensure.

Public regulation of any occupation or profession has as its basis protection of the public. Licensing provides a means of preventing people from offering services for which they do not have the prerequisite education or experience. It also provides a process for eliminating from an occupation or profession people whose personal character is not deserving of the public trust. However, no licensing process can ensure the quality of the work performed by a licensee; thus, any thought of using such a process to improve the quality of the service provided is misguided.

We talked earlier about moving to a professional practice model of schooling. In keeping with this philosophy, allowing the members of the education profession to determine who should practice it seems a proper direction to take. At the very least the profession should establish standards of performance for its members. Upon certification of acceptable performance by a professional standards board, state authorities then can license such persons, giving them the legal right to practice the profession. It is incumbent upon the professional standards board to establish and maintain high standards of professional practice. However, in the interest of public protection, the state legislature also may place other requirements upon persons seeking to practice the profession such as the absence of a criminal record or a state residence requirement.[5]

In a sense, all professions face the task of devising ways to document that someone is competent to practice the profession. In education there has been heavy reliance on academic preparation and a standardized test -- usually the National Teacher Examination (NTE) prepared by the Educational Testing Service. The recent emphasis on higher standards set by state legislatures and certification boards has raised the level of acceptable academic performance and NTE scores. The Educational Testing Service and others are developing more performance-based tests for novice teachers.[6] Nonetheless, there is considerable unrest about the suitability of these criteria as appropriate indicators.

Significant changes are needed in our teacher preparation programs to match the changes in teacher roles.

Colleges of education have debated these issues for several years. Various proposals for changing the academic preparation of teachers and administrators are currently under discussion. However, most of the discussion focuses on improving the preparation of people whose primary responsibility is to teach. As we move toward the goal of redesigning the classroom, schools will be looking for personnel with a different orientation. Significant changes are needed in our teacher preparation programs to match the changes in teacher roles.

Perhaps the right model for teacher preparation is the professional practice model on which the school itself is based. We tend to teach the way we are taught. It makes perfectly good sense, then, to have teachers learn in the same manner

---

their students are expected to learn. This means having clear teaching outcomes supported by appropriate learning activities. Much of the learning should be done in a technology environment similar to what students and teachers use in the local school. And college professors become mentors rather than lecturers.

Much of what teachers need to know and do in a learner-based method of schooling is best learned in the schoolhouse and not the university. After learning the knowledge base for the particular area of specialty, teachers can benefit greatly from working with other teachers as mentors. Whether this is part of the academic curriculum or takes the form of an internship is a matter for the profession to decide. "Book learning" is not in itself an appropriate preparation for mentoring the learning of others.

Notes to Chapter Five

1.   Carnegie Forum on Education and the Economy, *A Nation Prepared: Teachers for the 21st Century*. (New York: Carnegie Corporation of New York, 1986), p. 12.

2.   *Tomorrow's Teachers: A Report of the Holmes Group* (E. Lansing, MI: Holmes Group, Inc., 1986).

3.   In Kentucky the teacher membership on the School Council is elected by the certified staff according to a process established by local school district policy. The school principal or lead teacher must be a member. Statutorily, the Council membership consists of the school principal or lead teacher, three teachers and two parents of children in the school elected by the largest parent organization at the school. However, other configurations are possible with permission of the state Commissioner of Education.

4.   For an interesting discussion of this new occupational role, see Marvin J. Cetron, Barbara Soriano, and Margaret Gayle, "Schools of the Future: Education Approaches the Twenty-First Century," *The Futurist* August 1985, p. 22.

5.   Professional standards boards for educators are now being adopted by many states including Kentucky. However, the distinction between certifying that individuals are qualified to practice the profession and the act of granting them the legal right to practice remains a point of confusion. In most states these are one and the same, which may not properly balance the state's obligation to protect the public and the profession's obligation to set high standards of performance for itself without governmental interference.

6.   Connecticut has been working for several years on performance-based tests for novice teachers and is currently pilot testing one in mathematics. Other research and development efforts of a similar nature can be expected in future years.

Six

A SCHOOL
IN CONTEXT

The public school system in America is a creation of state governments. Each school operates as part of a larger system of education. State policymakers are the only ones in a position to implement broad-based system-wide change. However, significant changes in public policy are needed before schools can be redesigned. As the years have passed, more decisions about education have been made in the statehouse than in the schoolhouse. Vesting more responsibility for educational decisions with educators at the school site is a significant change in state policy.

The transition to an outcome-based school system necessitates changes in state accountability policy. The public accountability structure has to be based on student outcomes rather than on compliance with system input and process regulations. This means eliminating laws that stipulate the number of hours to be devoted to specific subjects, textbooks to be used, class sizes and other instructional directives. It also means more clearly defining the desired results and finding much better ways to document them. After many years of direct intervention in education, some lawmakers will find it

---

difficult to retreat from their proactive role in this arena. Shifts of this magnitude in state policy do not come easy.

A growing number of policymakers and others are urging educators to redesign their schools, but one can sense a real reluctance to singularly entrust the future of schools to teachers and administrators without some clear way to assess the effectiveness of their work. On the one hand, there is concern that educators will not respond in the way expected unless policymakers directly enforce their will through legislative mandate. On the other hand, efforts to mandate instructional activities are in conflict with a professional practice model of school management and impair the ability of schools to individualize education.

Building Accountability into the Education System

A public accountability system is based on assumptions about how external forces influence organizational behavior. An external accountability system presumes that (1) the members of an organization give attention to things that are likely to be inspected by someone *if* (2) the outcome of these inspections has meaningful consequences for the organization or its members. Given these assumptions, an education accountability system has to include systematic, valid methods of "inspecting" educational outcomes and an array of consequences that are meaningful enough to school personnel that they will take the desired action. In other words, the accountability system has to make the performance assessments a "high-stakes" process for everyone involved.

Bureaucratic management of complex organizations is based on the notion that people "at the top" determine the actions to be taken and people "at the bottom" are responsible for correctly implementing these actions. Results are what people at the top expect to happen if the actions they order are properly carried out. Therefore, when the expected results do not occur, either the actions ordered were wrong or they were not properly carried out. Accountability at the operational level of a bureaucracy is determining if people are properly following the directives given by management.

Bureaucracies try to ensure proper implementation by close supervision and inspection of work. Compliance with instructions about how work is to be carried out is central to the process. Workers in bureaucracies respond to the inspection of their work by paying careful attention to *how* things are done rather than *why* they are done. The "why" is a matter of outcomes determined by someone else. Rules, procedures and directives rather than purposiveness or judgment control their actions -- precisely what the accountability system intended. People who do their work in the manner they are told to do it will get the approval of their supervisors and management.

Accountability in our public education system has followed similar bureaucratic principles. Policymakers determine what they believe will work and then enact legislation or regulations directing the organization to conduct its business in a certain manner. School personnel are then held accountable for properly carrying out their directives. Therefore, educational accountability consists primarily of educators "accounting" to policymakers regarding their compliance with these laws and regulations.

It should be obvious that significant changes in our approach to educational accountability are a necessary part of redesigning the system of public education. The political and policy issues of accountability center on what is inspected, how it is inspected, and what consequences follow the inspection. Let's talk first about what is expected and how policymakers at all levels can know if it is being achieved; then we can think about consequences.

What is to be Inspected

A professional practice model of school organization requires methods of accountability different from those found in bureaucracies. Desired outcomes are agreed upon and professional performance is measured against these outcomes. An outcome-based accountability system requires clear understanding of what the outcomes are and how they can be documented. How the outcomes are achieved is important to professional educators, but the public accountability concern is that their professional practices be appropriate and efficacious.

The organizational "outcome" for a school is the learning demonstrated by its students. The idea of holding schools accountable for student learning originated when state legislators became concerned about a perceived decline in student achievement. Wanting to know how good their schools were, legislatures enacted laws requiring statewide student achievement testing. The results were controversial but informative. In the 1980s, accountability took an important turn. States like South Carolina, New Jersey and Kentucky required their Departments of Education to *intervene* in school districts that failed to meet certain performance standards including student scores on nationally normed tests.

A complete accountability system begins with students, parents and the local community. At the school site, accountability consists of daily and weekly assessments of each child's progress toward mastery of the various learning objectives. The learning objectives define the level of performance expected at specific points in the educational program. (Kentucky has selected grades 4, 8 and 12 as the threshold points.) Teachers (or mentors) regularly report this progress to students and parents according to local school board policy.

The Need for Better Assessment Methods

As we press for more esoteric learning outcomes such as the ability to communicate effectively, to think critically, to reason and solve problems, and to integrate and intelligently use knowledge, the more we realize how necessary it is that we bring about major reform in the way we attempt to document learning. It is generally agreed that the pencil and paper methodologies used in the past for state accountability testing do not capture many of the things we want children to know and be able to do. Clearly we must have more holistic, flexible and creative approaches to documenting learning than are typically found in state assessment programs today.

An innovative approach to the assessment of learning that can integrate both our instuctional and accountability objectives is to base both of them on a set of complex tasks designed to document attainment of specific learning objectives. The assessment tasks would be authentic performances that accurately reflect how students develop, understand and use knowledge as well as confirm their possession of specific information and skills. Documentation of the learning can take many forms -- portfolios, experiments, video and audio tapes, reenactments, exhibits and performances before a panel of judges.

The assessment tasks could measure multiple learning objectives and require higher levels of thinking than are demanded by most paper and pencil type examinations. The state could create prototypes of complex tasks that students can perform to demonstrate all of these objectives in an interactive context. A variety of tasks emulating the prototypes can be constructed that students can use to document their own learning. The state can approve these tasks for state assessment purposes as well. Assessments of this type would be rich, meaningful and exciting for students. Doing the tasks themselves could be a powerful learning exercise.

The State Inspection Process

An assessment of the performance of *schools* can be based in part on the performance of their students, but there must be a methodology for determining school effectiveness. Assuming the scenario given above for assessing *student* performance, one could expect schools to document that all students at the benchmark grade level can perform at the appropriate level of expertise any or all of the state-approved assessment tasks. Since teachers are regularly reporting this information to students and parents, there should be little problem in making the same information available to the state.

The assessment tasks students have been performing regularly as part of their classroom demonstrations are emulations of the state prototypes and are state approved. Since the assessment tasks are virtually the same there is no reason to require an independent demonstration of what the students have been doing regularly in the classroom. The issue here is whether one chooses to inspect the *student* and/or the *record of the student* in a state accountability program.

I believe it is important that we use the same methods of inspection for state purposes as are used for reporting to the student and parent. There should be no discrepancy between the feedback the student and parent have been getting about the student's performance and what would be learned from an independent assessment of that performance administered by the state. The status of every student should be known at all times, not after a state-administered test is given. The state accountability system should serve to validate the local assessments and not contradict them.

The primary reason for separate testing is a general distrust of report card grades, not a belief that such tests are a superior method of documenting learning. The state can regularly audit the documentation on which student assessments are based at the school site level. The assessments made by the school staff can be evaluated by the auditors against state-established standards. The auditors can issue a public report on their findings much like public accountants do after a financial audit. If there are important discrepancies the state can conduct an inquiry to determine the reasons.

Accountability by auditing ongoing student performance rather than direct student testing can increase the value of the local assessment process by giving it more credibility. It also increases the importance of regular student assessments and avoids the necessity of a separate statewide examination. Finally, the audit process can provide an opportunity for improving the quality of local assessments and can help achieve over time a shared understanding among teachers of what constitutes acceptable student performance.

The frequency of the audits and the personnel used to perform them are matters for policymakers to determine. As for the integrity of the accountability process, the assessment data reported to the state are based on information being given to students and parents. They can be taken at face value until an audit turns up evidence that the reporting is inaccurate. In the event of an "audit exception" state authorities can be required to take whatever action is thought necessary to determine the actual status of the students in the school. Should the discrepancies be due to fraudulent behavior, there is probable cause for professional and legal action against the parties responsible.

What Constitutes Acceptable School Performance

School effectiveness should no longer be based on the average performance of all students in a school, but on the *proportion* of all students attaining a high level of performance on the designated outcomes. In a world where "quality" has come to mean "zero defects," policymakers are not interested any

---

longer in how students *as a group* are doing "on the average." They want to know how near we are to having *all* students learning at the highest level of which they are capable.

As we press for high performance from every student, we must incorporate in the accountability system measures that deter schools from pushing the poorer performing students out or deliberately holding them back in order to improve the school's performance record. The Kentucky system holds schools accountable for keeping children in school and advancing through their entire academic program on schedule. Rewards cannot be earned, nor intervention be avoided, at the expense of the children.

Kentucky defined school effectiveness in terms of the proportion of students who are successful in attaining all the learning objectives set for their learning level. Schools are required to meet certain *improvement* goals every two years that include an increase in the proportion of students who perform at the threshold level, maintain a desired level of attendance and remain in school. The State Board for Elementary and Secondary Education establishes the improvement goals for each school site every two years.

The Kentucky Department of Education will help teachers create a broad array of classroom experiences through which students can develop the skills and knowledge required to successfully perform the assessment tasks. Staff at the school-site level are given great freedom to organize their school resources and instructional practices in whatever way they believe is necessary to attain the desired student outcomes.

Although it is naive to think schools will not be ranked according to their "performance score," Kentucky is making a conscious effort to avoid such comparisons. Every school is expected to improve its effectiveness as measured against its own previous best effort. Awards and interventions are based upon the *improvement* made irrespective of the actual level of effectiveness demonstrated. If every school improves each year, the whole system will be better regardless of the actual level of performance of any individual school.

Finally, making schools rather than school districts the unit of accountability places the responsibility for improvement in student performance at the level where it matters most. Many school districts that are perceived to be "good" have poor performing schools in them. There is little incentive to improve those schools. Measuring the effectiveness of every school will provide an incentive to these districts to improve all their schools and thus improve the educational opportunity of all children regardless of the community or neighborhood in which they live.

Enhancing the Consequences

State policymakers are showing great interest in finding equitable and meaningful ways to enhance the consequences attached to the school accountability system. Under its new school law, Kentucky schools that show steady improvement will receive cash awards to be used as the majority of faculty in the school determines. A school that fails to improve or actually declines in the proportion of students who attain the expected level of performance will be declared a "school in crisis." The faculty and administration of such a school will be subject to transfer or dismissal based on an outside evaluation, and parents can request that their children be transferred to a more successful school of the superintendent's choice.

An accountability system can constructively reinforce desired organizational behavior if such outcomes are anticipated in its design. In the Kentucky approach there is an emphasis upon a team effort and collective accountability. The cash awards can only be earned as a school. Furthermore, exemplary individual effort will not keep a teacher from being placed on probation if the school is declared to be "in crisis."

The professional effectiveness of other teachers now becomes a matter of personal consequence and mutual concern.

The Relationship Between Accountability and Instruction

As policymakers seek for better ways to hold schools accountable, they need to realize how much statewide accountability tests influence instruction. Experience shows that teachers will "teach to the test" if the outcomes of such tests are interpreted as a reflection of their competence. Teachers will teach what these tests measure so long as their results are publicly scrutinized and school "quality" is measured by them. One cannot stress too much the importance of adopting assessment methodologies that can better document the kind of outcomes the public truly values.

Since what we inspect and reward has a direct bearing on what is taught, the kinds of outcomes we choose to measure and the methods we use to measure them will most certainly shape what our children will learn in our schools. Therefore, the kind of accountability system we create will likely have a more direct and immediate effect on the nature and focus of schooling than any other action we will take and may very well constitute the most significant aspect of our effort to redesign public schools.

What Lies Ahead?

The situation we find ourselves in reminds me of a sight we all have seen at one time or another as we travel our interstate highways:

> CONSTRUCTION AHEAD
> TRAFFIC MAINTAINED
> PROCEED WITH CAUTION

Detour signs, orange drums, dust and rough road are part of every highway construction scene. As we begin work on our new kind of school, keep in mind that it must be built while we "maintain traffic" on the old. There will be inconveniences, delays, messy conditions at times and detours for some. The alternative is to close down the road until a new one is completed -- an option that really doesn't exist in this case.

There is a limit to the reach of a state legislature or a policy board like a state board of education. Most of what needs to happen to convert our schools into learning institutions requires the support and participation of thousands of teachers who now control what goes on in the classroom. We are seeking a fundamental change in what people do in our schools. We want to change what teachers do professionally. Change takes people into the unknown and they are fearful. In fact, fear may be the most formidable obstacle we will face in our effort to change schools. *Not fear - maybe Paradigmns*

Fear for some comes from an uncertainty that the alternative really can work the way we say it will. Others are fearful of how it may affect their children or how much it might cost. Still others fear their careers are in jeopardy. Some changes in the past have been very traumatic, especially the consolidation of small schools, racial integration and forced busing of children. Even modest changes are not always well received. We can expect many of those responsible for our schools to be very cool toward the kind of changes proposed here.

School administrators and board members are cautious for good reasons. Change in the past often has meant law suits, disruption of school routine, noisy board meetings, angry parents and sometimes loss of a job. Experience with change has taught them that it generally yields low returns. It is best to leave things alone. "If it ain't broke, don't fix it," is their motto.

As someone once put it, we are already too late to be early. If we change our schools today, the year 2000 will pass by the time the first students to complete the new curriculum are graduated from secondary school! For these students, the 21st century is now. We should delay no longer in the pursuit of a better approach to schooling our young. The future of this great nation depends on our ability to compete intellectually, socially, economically and politically with other nations of the world -- something we may be unable to do unless we soon find a way to better prepare *all* our people for the kind of world that is emerging. Making a new kind of school could be the single most important thing we can contribute in the struggle to preserve our nation and our way of life.

About the Author

Jack D. Foster received his doctorate in sociology from The Ohio State University. He presently serves as Governor Wallace G. Wilkinson's Secretary of Education and Humanities for the Commonwealth of Kentucky. Prior to his current position, Dr. Foster was a public policy researcher and consultant, university professor and department chairman, and protestant clergyman. He has a broad background in the fields of social psychology, theology, criminal justice and education. During the 1980s, he assisted Governors William F. Winter (Mississippi), Robert D. Orr (Indiana), and Wallace G. Wilkinson (Kentucky) in education policy reform. He resides in Lexington, Kentucky.